14 THINGS RICH DO THAT POOR DON'T

Andrew Palmer

Copyright © 2018 Andrew Palmer
All rights reserved.
ISBN: 9781719904728

DEDICATION

Dedication, dedication is what you need if you want to get to the top and want to be the cream of the crop. Dedication is what you need.

CONTENTS

Introduction

Buy used stuff (cars), most of the time	7
Reading	9
TV Argghh No	11
Bills that get paid by skills	13
Investing is interesting	14
Budget	15
Mingle with the Jingle	16
Living like the poor	17
What a goal	18
Mistakes learn from them	19
Don't be tempted by fool's gold	20
Eat right	21
Rich people focus on opportunities Rich grow larger than their problems	22

INTRODUCTION

Me curious about the rich no never he gasps. Ok yes I have been a bit teeny weeny bit curious by the wealthy. Jealousy plays no part in this Ahem Ahem I have always wondered how some of them keep their wealth.

14 Things rich do that poor don't. Is a funny sentence it's so nonsensical its even grammatically challenged. Here you are on the next page chomping at the bit wondering what makes the rich tick. How do they become rich? What do they do to maintain that flash car and designer clothes?

I do know a few people that are wealthy, and no this book is not based on you. This book is based on my research. Which consisted of me basically hanging out in the members area of London clubs with footballers (if your names not down ya not coming in. Chilling out with stockbrokers and wealthy business people whether it be at the golf range or just playing Fortnite on Xbox.

This book will give you 14 reasons why the rich stay rich game and the rest of us try to keep it real.

BUY USED STUFF (CARS), MOST OF THE TIME

The rich, the wealthy among us do have a lot of money and because of this us folk think that they buy everything new. When actual fact They don't. Yes they use cashback sites and coupons. This helps them to keep a balance and not just monetary. Rich people have a knack of knowing where and how much money should be spent. Most of the time they will, only spend money to make heaps more money.

A typical example of this is a new car. Most of those that are rich will not buy a new car. A new car loses 20% and can lose up to 35% within 2-3 years of its value as soon as you drive it off the forecourt. This is called depreciation which the rich don't have an appreciation for. By buying a car that is just a year old you can save a few thousand.

The "real rich" do drive 10-year old Honda Civics or Toyota Camrys. It has been highlighted by an Experian Automotive study that 61% of wealthy people drive Toyotas, Hondas and Fords. Stop Acting rich author wrote a piece that the middle ground price for what millionaires paid for their cars was $31,367. Those that spend their money at the wealthy brand car makers have very little wealth to show for it. Unless you are in the middle east that is.

Using the term "wealth", gives those that have it a name to show how much they are worth. When all is said and done, those that purchase expensive luxury cars are those with higher levels of income. This does not necessarily mean bought by those who are wealthy, or loaded. You see your income is a lot different than wealth..

READING

Rich people read yes you heard me they read!

They will read anything from anywhere. It can be anything from the news, financial papers, self-improvement books, vegan recipes, and they have even read 14 things rich do that poor don't

Rich people read to learn. They are constantly reading, but not just any reading material. Anything that interest them the gives them a different perspective.

Audio books have been become so popular to the rich as these types of books helps them multi-task. Making money means more free time and free time means make more money

Just remember this, I am not saying the not so rich do not read. I am saying the rich do read more often. It's just good to read articles related to you career aspirations. Research shows that 88% of rich people will read at minimum 30 minutes each day, while only 2% of the poor don't.

"lifelong educational self-improvement gives me more of a chance of being wealthy, something I truly believe in is, reading." ~ Andrew Palmer.

63% of wealthy parents make their children read two or more non-fiction books a month vs. 3% of poor?

As of 2017, I like to read a good investment book. I will often have my words of wisdom soundbites from the late great Bob Marley in my earphones even whilst writing a book.

TV ARGGHH NO

Time is money this is the number one thing rich people advocate. Television (tell Lie Vision) is where rich people will draw the line. Poor people will spend a lot of their lives watching the TV. Whether they are at home or coming home from a job. Soaps and TV series are those most watched. You won't find rich people watching Eastenders or Love and Hip Hop. What are they doing? Yep you guessed it; the rich are productive, and like I said in chapter before they are reading.

As well as watching not watching TV you won't find them on social on social media apps, commenting on Instagram about flowers.

"Whilst I get rich of learning from my large collection of books, poor people get a large amounts of followers on insta." ~ Andrew Palmer

BILLS THAT GET PAID BY SKILLS

Learning new skills comes with the territory of being rich. A lot of rich people can speak several language particularly the language of foreign currency.

Rich people are always on the lookout how can I make money from a different pathway or new skill. It's about creating revenue streams from different avenues. Making money and generating profit from those skill sets.

Where ever a rich person smell money they will find a way to get it. For instance, you want two ice creams from one note which isn't enough. The poor will just go spend the note on one ice cream and have no change. The rich person mentality is to go get water and lemon make lemonade, sell it and then they have more money to buy two ice creams.

INVESTING IS INTERESTING

Now we this is where things get real interesting. The people you see that you hear of that are rich. What do you think one of the single most important things that they do is? They rich because Rich people invest. If it makes money now or long term and they can see a long term profit they will invest in gold, real estate, artwork and other business. These investments are both intangible and tangible items.

I have tried to be saver all my life and I haven't been the greatest at it but what I know is I am investing in properties and other business. I see these as a profitable long-term income.

All successful people who have invested will never put all their eggs in a basket. That would be suicidal. You have to spread it across your portfolio

BUDGET

Budgeting means you have to set aside some money and stick to it. It doesn't matter if your buying something for small change or bigger purchase stick to your budget. This is one of best ways rich people have kept what they got.

Track your money and save. Without fail Rich people come up with ingenious ways to stick to their budget. This not spending over the odds or cost for something means rich people have a inner strength not to budge no matter how tempting. Rich people will look at the calendar each week, month, even day and know exactly where their money is

When I was younger I found it hard to budget even though I was a bit of a spendthrift. Yep I would never treat myself and always look out for others. Now I have invested and earning a bit each month. I can allow myself the freedom to spend a bit more on a vegan cake mwahahahhah

MINGLE WITH THE JINGLE

As the title of this chapter would suggest mix with people with money. The richer they are the better for you to get jiggy with. Network and surround yourself with wealthy people, with a wealthy mindset. Poor people fail to do this they keep themselves down with the wrong mindset.

Of course, not everyone who is poor will get that chance to be around people who are in a higher wealth bracket as them. Also when I say rich I am saying mingle and talk to someone who may be in higher paid job than you.

Also you might find that not all is as it seems sometimes you could have friends or associates that are rich but you don't know it. That's why if you want to become rich it's good that you have a certain mindset. As I will reveal in the next chapter.

LIVING LIKE THE POOR

I bet you didn't know there are a lot of Millionaires amongst us and a lot of them you might not recognise as rich. These people live cleverly and think intelligently. They are choosing to live within their means and rather than flaunt their wealth they would rather keep it under wraps. You will probably be saying with clenched teeth of course it's easy if you are a millionaire to live that way. I still think it's about having a fixed mind set the richer you become the harder it is to give into the urges and splurges.

Point is you may have far less now than anyone at the moment even if you have far less, its best to get into a habit of not spending or just spending small. I am telling you to do this do you want more is less or "less is more" ?

Ask yourself a question have you ever met a person that you thought this person doesn't have two coins to rub together. Then you find out that person has a lot of money. Yep, they are around you every day.

WHAT A GOAL!

.
Have you ever dreamed of retirement? Have you ever dreamed of living on a beach, somewhere in the sun? Have you ever dreamed of owning a Rolls Royce wraith? Tinted windows and all decked out in black. Cruising down the highway listening to...ooops sorry that's my dream.

Let me tell you rich people set long-term goals. Setting long-term goals is paramount for you to be able to save.

Rich people tend to look far into the future which is part of their strategy to have as much money as they can for their retirement fund.

I know that I want to have money saved for retirement, It can be hard to understand for any of us how much we need.

MISTAKES LEARN FROM THEM

You can make mistakes and you will but do you have to? Rich people budget and do a lot of planning rich people are calculated and very meticulous and by nature very calculated.

They educate themselves as much as possible so Reducing risk in their every move is very important hence reading a lot of things

Rich people are prone to make mistakes, as we have seen throughout life. The difference is yes it may prove costlier, but they are less likely to make those mistakes again.

If your good at one thing and making money of it stick to it The name of the game is not what you know but who.

Don't be Tempted by Fool's Gold

We are constantly bombarded with so many tempting things. We are tempted to live the high life and big ourselves up. The temptation to live beyond our means is everywhere. Our so-called friends, colleagues, and the temptation to keep up with 'them next door'.

The pressure can be unbearable, but like I said before it's not impossible to have a mind set to watch what others have with envy. Over spending and miscalculation is detrimental to your health and well-being short term and long term.

That means going cold turkey: Avoid malls, unsubscribe from all those retail emails and don't sign up for new ones and say "no" to invitations that you know will cost you. Force yourself to avoid negative financial influences as much as possible.

Then, replace these temptations with things that motivate you.

EAT RIGHT

Poor people tend to eat junk food and food that is not good for you. People will say well that is understandable as rich eat better or more. The rich are able to eat better yes but because your poor doesn't mean that you have to. Fruits and vegetables are so important and don't hardly cost anything. So look what I did just then I made you think rich. Rich people tend to stay away from fruits and vegetables but will indulge themselves on food like different types of meat. Which long-term yes they eating well now but will lead to adverse health.

Food for thought for the day 70 per cent of wealthy people eat less than 300 junk food calories each day. Yes, 97 per cent of poor people eat more than 300 junk food calories per day.

RICH PEOPLE FOCUS ON OPPORTUNITIES

There was a shoe salesperson that found himself in a country, trying to sell shoes to the locals. The only problem was, nobody there wore shoes. The salesman soon gave up in frustration and decided to leave the area. On his way out, he met another shoe salesman. "Don't bother entering this town," said the first person, "These people don't wear shoes." The second salesperson eyes grew wide, "Nobody has shoes? Wow I could sell a pair to everyone in town! An untapped market how fortune favours the brave.

Perception is key!

RICH GROW LARGER THAN PROBLEMS

Poor people see a problem and immediately recognize it as bad luck or 'it had to happen to me' then they quit trying. The rich do run into problems and then look for a way to solve it and focus on the positives, and they don't give up.

Rich people will keep pushing and pushing until they get the end result and if all is lost they will try something else.

Acknowledgements

Thanks to all those that are still in my life right now.
Getting rich is just around the corner stick with me!

ABOUT THE AUTHOR

ANDREW PALMER A 'PHOENIX FROM THE FLAMES' IS CURRENTLY WRITING A SERIES OF BOOKS HAVING BEEN A SUCCESSFUL ENTREPRENEUR FOR MANY YEARS

7+1 STEPS TO STARING YOUR OWN GRIND
is the
No.1 bestseller on the Apple itunes store

www.ingramcontent.com/pod-product-compliance
Lightning Source LLC
Chambersburg PA
CBHW030042230526
45472CB00002B/630